The Gift of Spells

Open the door to a world of magick, spiritual empowerment and happiness

LUCY CAVENDISH

ROCKPOOL
PUBLISHING

A Rockpool book
PO Box 252
Summer Hill
NSW 2130
Australia
www.rockpoolpublishing.com.au
www.facebook.com/RockpoolPublishing

ISBN 978-1-925429-37-4

First published in 2013 by Rockpool Publishing as
Spellbound ISBN 978-1-925017-15-1.
This edition published in 2019

Design by Trenett Ha, Rockpool Publishing
Images by Shutterstock
Printed and bound in China

10 9 8 7 6 5 4 3 2 1

Contents

Welcome to the
Craft of Spellcasting

What is a Spell?

There is an immense natural power in the Universe which you are a part of. You were born with this natural power. What our modern world has done is harness these natural powers in many ways – electricity, solar power, digital technology – but there is a deep, deep force that has not been harnessed, which cannot be controlled, which flows through all of us. Why don't you feel this force? Because most modern humans are completely disconnected from their own power. And the secrets to working with this power have almost been lost.

Spells are a way of reintroducing you to that natural power that flows through everything, including you. Crafting and casting spells will help reintroduce you to that power source, reconnect you, and that powerful connection with natural energy will help you create a meaningful, magickal life.

What is Magick?

Magick is the art and the craft and the philosophy of understanding nature's powers and then working with those powers to create the results you want and deserve in your life. That means bending and shaping natural forces. It does not mean trapping them, or distorting them, or exploiting them. Magick has many laws and many rules. But the most important truth about magick is that you are a living example of magick. Yes, you! Without a whole series of natural amazing forces, right timing, fate, destiny and cosmic alignments, you would not exist. And there has never been anyone just like you – not any time before, now, or ever again. You are a natural miracle. You are magick.

Bending and Shaping your Energy Wisely

There are laws and rules that apply to magick and spellcasting. But don't ever let the fact that there are rules and laws stop you from casting! People can be fearful of spellwork as they worry about a natural kind of punishment or that they are playing with an energy they cannot control. This notion comes from those age-old religions who tell you that fire and brimstone will rain down on you if you are not 'good', all backed up by the myths put out by so very many films and the media. You have this natural power within you, and it is your birthright to learn how to work with it.

Rules and Laws of Magick and Witchcraft

The Law of the Threefold Return. This law states that what you send out will return to you multiplied times three. This is called the law of the threefold return. Therefore, we do not cast with unhealthy energy because that is how you are going to feel, three times as much as the person or situation you're sending it to.

Be balanced when you cast. The most important energetic law when preparing to spellcast is to be clean and clear in your energy. No matter how angry or upset you are, you always need to be in a state of balance and calm when you cast. What this means is no drugs, alcohol or coffee before casting – you want your connection to be clean. If your energy is not clear, your spell won't be either.

The Law of Harm None. Doctors have this oath, and as spellcrafting is a kind of healing, and definitely a working with natural energy to create change in accordance with the will, it is not surprising that as we know how to use these powers, we make a promise that when we use them, we will do no harm. What this law means is no casting to harm or hurt, no matter what. Before you cast, always say to yourself, 'harm none'. There is a famous magickal saying: an it harm none, do what ye will. Let that be your guide.

Cast for the Highest Good of all concerned. These words are often woven into a spell, in order to ask the Universe to help the casting be of the greatest possible good to all who are going to be affected by the spell.

Love is the Law. If we are not going to do any harm, and if we truly wish for the Highest Good of all concerned, that means Love is the law. Love of life, of ourselves, of the planet, of the Deities, of the sheer visceral thrill of being alive. So, where does this leave the infamous cursing and hexing? Many Witches do hex – it can be an effective way to stop something that is worth this risky magick. Hexing can work with 'inanimate' objects – hexing a disease is one practice some Witches feel very comfortable with. For our purposes here, we will first work with ways to banish, block, protect and change energy – without hexing. You will learn of magickal practices which deactivate the impact of negative people and improve difficult situations. These practices won't hurt the person. You'll be taught to deflect your attention away from the person and turn the magick so it affects behaviour – including your own, which will be making a significant energetic contribution to the situation. You'll learn some strong, fast-working psychic self-defence moves too. These are fun, empowering and, most importantly, effective.

The Law of Free Will. When we cast, we never cast to interfere with another person's free will. So, for example, we do not cast to persuade someone to do something against their will. This is magickal malpractice, and yet it is frequently sought after. Never cast without another person's consent. Do not cast to get people back together against the will of one of the people involved. Another ground rule is to never cast a spell or send energies to another person without their consent. Even if you mean well and are sending good energy or 'light' – it is an invasion of a person's spiritual space. Obey this law, and you will cast safely and effectively for many years to come.

Like attracts Like. What we think, we become. What we believe, we create. What we work with in our spells, we develop an affinity for, and a relationship with. If we wish to work magick, we must work with tools and ingredients that are like that which we wish to create or attract. This law has been renamed in recent years, and is often referred to as the law of attraction. We attract what we are. Our energy dictates our experience. This is not new. It is ancient, and it is powerful.

Never cast for negative outcomes. If you begin casting for vengeful, malicious, petty and especially spiteful, egoistic reasons, the impact is rarely pretty – for anyone. If you make this your practice you will take the brunt of the effect of the spell. Your energy will become drained and your faith in your magickal practice and in yourself will be severely shaken.

These laws can daunt potential spellcasters fearful of making a mistake, who worry they may inadvertently create mayhem. Gently place those fears and anxieties aside. Together we can travel right inside the magick of the Universe, and learn to understand natural energies so you have the best possible spellcasting experiences. But you need to make a promise to devote some time to work out why you want what you think you want. You need to understand the energy around you and how you can bend and shape it with wisdom. Spellcasting is not

a matter of dipping in, casting a spell, life is perfect. It's more a matter of understanding the energy and tapping into its powerful force to help you create your own special magick. A big key to tapping into this energy is being open and learning to see your world differently. Magickally you will learn to open your heart and your eyes to the wider world.

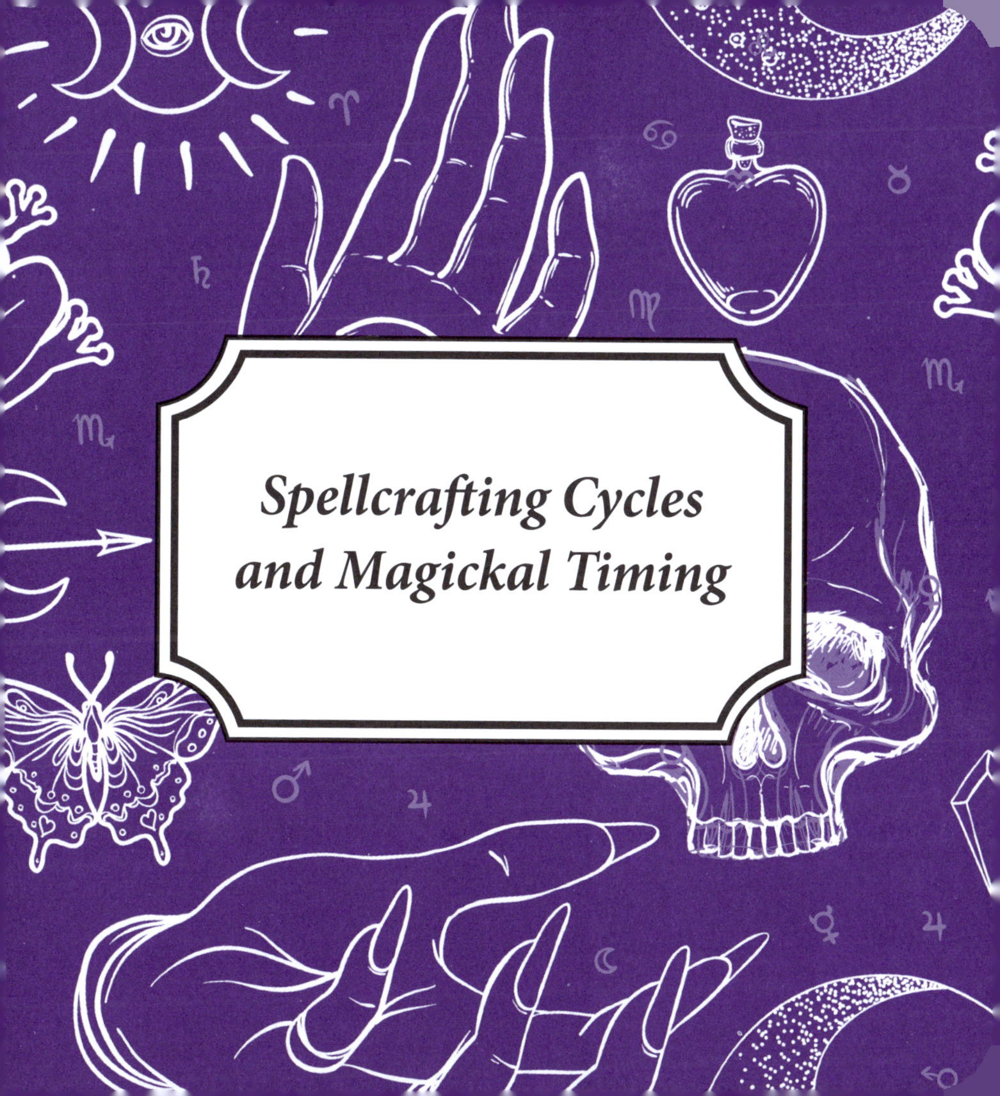

Spellcrafting Cycles and Magickal Timing

The Timing of Spellcrafting and Casting

A great proportion of effective spellcrafting and casting is knowing when to cast for what it is you want to create in your life. It's a little like being a great gardener – gardeners who are really talented and tuned in and knowledgeable do not try to grow jasmine in autumn or pumpkins in springtime. Spells work not because you're doing anything unnatural, they work because you're fertilising the possibilities the natural energy cycles are giving you. You're not going to try and work against nature – you're going to work WITH her – with her timing and cycles, and this is going to enhance the impact of your casting.

Whenever you are preparing for your spellcasting, have a look at moon charts and write down in your Grimoire the time you have done your spells so you can see what times have worked and what times have not.

Casting by the Moon

Lunar phases have long been observed and held sacred. We have watched the tides ebb and flow, witnessed the response of the plants to the moonlight, and noticed people's behaviour change at different phases of the lunar cycle.

When we craft and cast spells, we nearly always do so at a time that is going to support the intentions and the purpose of the spell. There are important phases of each lunar cycle which we work with.

Dark Moon. This is the brief phase during which there is no visible moon in the night sky. The moon is always there, but at this phase, she is not discernible to the human eye as she is turned away from the light of the sun. Dark moon is especially revered in many countries for cleansing rituals. The darkness brings up all that needs to be released, or ended, or completed, before going into the next phase, that of beginnings and new growth.

Cast for: Spells involving going deep within, working with the aspects of yourself you wish to learn more about, banishing, clearing, and deep, lasting protection. Understanding mysteries, connecting with deities who are considered dark – sometimes called the Dark Mother. This lunar phase gives us an opportunity to discover what has been hidden. A wonderful time to ask for secrets to be revealed, to wind up relationships and to release old and unwanted habits.

New Moon. A new moon is when you can see that very fine silver crescent light up the night sky. The new moon is all about a building, a gathering of energy and it is the time to start to sow the seeds of new projects, initiate ideas and relationships. It is the time to make a romantic advance, to initiate an exercise program. The energy at this time supports beginnings.

Cast for: Spells to begin a project, land a job, draw a new love, find a new home. Generally, it is the right time to make any kind of change. It is gentle energy, so you must give any spell you work at new moon time to work before you see strong results.

Waxing Moon. This is not a phase, but a term used to describe the moon as she grows from dark to full – she waxes, grows bigger.

Waxing Quarter Moon. This is a phase when establishment, building and solidifying can take place. We can really begin to see results, and observe growth by putting even more effort into our desires. At this stage, what we have cast for at the new moon will be growing, establishing itself and showing signs of manifesting.

Cast for: Building on the energy of new moon work or spells, reinvigorate current projects, for work, abundance, increase and commitment to relationships.

Waxing Gibbous. This is the time between the waxing first quarter and the full moon. There may be obvious, fast growth, and more and more progress.

Cast for: Alliances, back-up, resources, storage, memory, provisions, expansion, evolution, progress, blossoming, extension.

Full Moon. This is the time of the 'High Tide of Power'. It is a time of fullness and intensity, when all that is being worked on, all that you are feeling and thinking and doing, will be amplified. It is very, very powerful. Some spiritual practitioners have suggested releasing at full moon. I strongly advise against this, as it is too volatile to release into. It is a time for fullness and, at such times, power can literally spill over.

Cast for: Increasing connection to lovers, gratitude, celebration, giving thanks, positive energy, divination, increase and amplification, generation of energy, absorbing energy as this is extremely replenishing.

Waning Gibbous. Now, after the full moon, it is time to let go, to hold parties, to enjoy physical activity and dancing. The time between the full moon and the waning quarter moon. This is a time when rapid clearing and release can take place, with very obvious results.

Cast for: Reduction, diminishment, transformation, transmutation, dissolving negativity and difficult issues, releasement, clearing, cleansing, banishing.

Waning Quarter Moon. This moon, like the first quarter moon, looks 'half full'. It will again be useful for sending away, it also is a kind of drawing out. So, releasing negativity, losing weight, changing poor habits are favoured as energy is moving out – the tide is sucking out – so it is a purifying and releasing time.

Cast for: Clearly it is the time to send, to send away, release, detox and purge. It is the time to clean house, clean up our act energetically, to let go of bad habits.

Waning Moon. This term describes the moon when it grows smaller - waning or diminishing in size, from full through to dark again.

Casting by the Wheel of the Year

Magick works with natural cycles of the earth and of the heavens. There are eight traditional festivals in modern magick. Four are associated with the changing of the seasons and four are connected to the Universe – two solstices, two equinoxes. Use these festivals as a guide to timing your spells. The Witches' Year is said to begin at Samhain, so this is where we will begin this guide to the Wheel of the Year.

Samhain (pronounced Sow-en)

31 October–1 November in the Northern Hemisphere
30 April–1 May in the Southern Hemisphere

This is the Witches' magickal New Year. It is the time of the ancestors, when ghosts walk with us and when we acknowledge and remember those who have gone before us. It is a time of harvest and a time to light the darkness, and we begin to make preparations for the cold times coming. It has been adopted by popular culture and is known as Halloween, a variation of the old name, All Hallows' Eve.

This is a strong time for candle magick, scrying, divination to forecast for the year ahead, and connecting with ancestors. It is also a perfect time to practise your mediumship skills.

Cast for: Finding a mentor, guide or benefactor, as older, wiser energies can be trapped at Samhain.

Winter Solstice – Yule

20–23 December in the Northern Hemisphere
20–23 June in the Southern Hemisphere

This is the longest night of the year – the time of the greatest darkness and of severe cold in many lands. The energy is slow, internalised and withdrawn. It is a time of incubation, hibernation and conserving energy. At the solstice, great celebrations were held through Northern Europe to call the sun back to life and warmth. Many ancient sacred sites were built to ritually honour and observe the solstices – and observation of the winter solstice, the time of rebirth after the death of the cold time, is considered by many to have been one of the primary purposes of Stonehenge. This is a time for candle magick, rebirthing, beginning the process of recovery after healing, divination for the future, gratitude and giving thanks.

Cast for: If you are feeling lost, for you to find your way through the darkness. Clearing of negativity and space clearing can also be worked with.

Imbolc

1–2 February in the Northern Hemisphere
1–2 August in the Southern Hemisphere

This is a festival of growth, mothering, young life and nurturing the tender newness of the coming spring. Imbolc is an old Gaelic word that means 'ewe's milk' which relates to the birth of baby animals at this time. It is a fresh, invigorating and blessed festival. Because of the newness there is an innocence and a heightened sensitivity to the energy. It has a pure, sweet quality.

Cast for: The future, new life, young ones, hopes, dreams, kindness and care, to be comforted, for mothers and parents, for teachers, counsellors and carers, change, education. To create optimism, self-love, tenderness and new romance.

Spring Equinox – Ostara

20–23 March in the Northern Hemisphere
20–23 September in the Southern Hemisphere

This is a traditional Northern Hemisphere and Nordic celebration of fertility, abundance and new life. It is named for and devoted to the Goddess Ostara. It is linked to maturation, development, coming of age and initiation and is a joyful, hopeful time. As it is an Equinox, the light and the dark are in perfect balance of equal duration, with the light growing stronger from the next day forth. So, it is a celebration, too, of warmth. Many of its ancient traditions have been worked into Christianity's rites of Easter – a direct reference to Ostara's name. The eggs, the hare who brings them, and the sweetness of chocolate and treats are all traditionally the gifts of this kind and lovely Nordic lunar Goddess.

Cast for: Emotional balance, anything at all to do with equality and fairness, sexuality, physical strength and fitness, health and wellbeing, justice, education, fair dealing, abundance, friendships, physical makeovers, beauty, gardening, attraction.

Beltane

30 April–1 May in the Northern Hemisphere
31 October–1 November in the Southern Hemisphere

This is the highly sexual fertility festival of the Ancient Celts, a festival that means 'bright fire' which will re-light the fire within you when you observe its magick. This is the traditional time for handfastings, or pagan weddings. It is a celebration of beauty, sensuality and desire. Beltane is a purifying festival. When, finally, the cold days had departed, animals could be moved into the higher paddocks to graze and spend time outdoors, bringing freedom and freshness. The fires that burned at this time lit up lovers meeting in the flower-filled fields. Today, as the world about you warms, you will feel inspired to dance, laugh and enjoy friendship and even fall in love.

Cast for: Attracting a love or lover who is committed and extremely attracted to you. To focus on your physicality, your health, your desirability and power. It is a time to dress up and play, rearrange your social life, make new friends and have flirtatious fun. It is a time of abundance, good fortune and prosperity. Spells cast to attract these will be highly favoured while Beltane's intoxicating energy holds sway.

Summer Solstice – Litha

20–23 June in the Northern Hemisphere
20–23 December in the Southern Hemisphere

This is the festival of the faeries – Litha is intensely joyous, celebratory and full of light. It celebrates and marks the longest day of the year and it gives us all the opportunity to relax, bathe in the warmth, have plenty of time to ourselves, to spend with friends, play music, dance and be enchanted by the full flower of summer. It is a festival that encourages us to slow down and relax, sunbathe, stretch and give thanks for the simple joy of being alive under summer skies.

Cast for: Physical strength and health, creativity, inspiration and friendships. Parties thrown at this time are all magickal. Good fortune is more easily activated and vitality and play are also encouraged. You will have strong connections to plants, trees and crystals. You are more telepathic at Litha, more relaxed, like a blossom opening to the sun. Take good care of yourself as there can be a tendency to overdo celebrations.

Lughnasad

1–2 August in the Northern Hemisphere
1–2 February in the Southern Hemisphere

As the dark lengthens, it is time to harvest and give thanks to the Universe for what we have created – to be grateful. This is a time of balancing the efforts we have made with the enjoyment of what we have created – to celebrate the light that remains, to make the most of every moment before darkness falls. It is when Lugh, the Celtic God of Light was honoured, and as he is also a God of many talents, we attempt to do as much as we can at this busy time. We enjoy the bounty of our good fortune at this time, but put what we need away for the cold times are ahead. We also share, because when we have good fortune, we must also share it with others. We also resolve disputes at Lughnasad.

Cast for: Destiny, height of maturity and growth, peaks and pinnacles, luxury and comfort, cleansing and preparation, planning. It is a time to consider your future, plan and get organised. And to mend relationships or end them peacefully.

Autumn Equinox – Mabon

20–23 September in the Northern Hemisphere
20–23 March in the Southern Hemisphere

This is the time of the descent into darkness, to strengthen ourselves: to make sure we are well, physically and mentally and to ready ourselves for Winter. As the dark grows and lengthens, there will be changes, even separations. We are asked to be more responsible, serious, earnest and honest with ourselves. We must become leaders, and to begin to think for ourselves, and to rely on others. This is a time of complexity, as the days have this one last moment of balance, before the dark consumes the light once again.

Cast for: Dedication, energy, independence, intelligence, practicality, study, qualifications, self-improvement, higher standards and making peace. It is a time for justice, to air grievances and to be sure we know where we stand with others before making commitments.

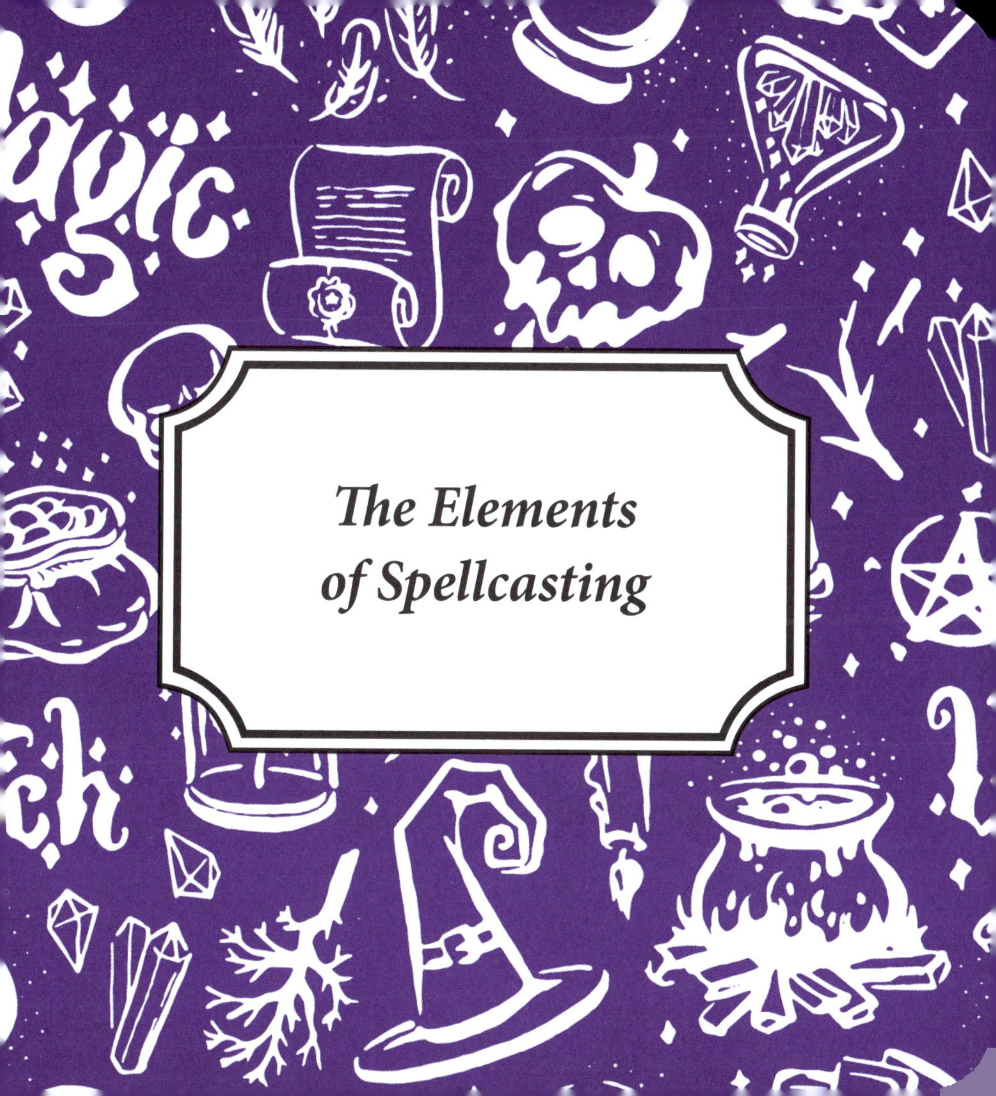

The Elements of Spellcasting

Building a Magickal Altar

Magick brings us closer to the pure beating heart of your world, our world, the whole world. The closer you are to feeling that primal heartbeat the juicier, the keener, the tastier life gets. Spellwork creates a connection to the planet that makes you realise you belong. You feel safe, at home and protected. You will worry less about what others think and feel about you – you won't lose empathy, and you won't stop caring, but you will stop worrying over issues that truly are a major drain on your life force. And that means you can achieve great things in your life.

It is a powerful magickal exercise to build an altar, using objects that you find or collect. Be intuitive about this process. While it's great to collect a symbol for each element: earth, air, fire, water, spirit, it's more important that everything says something about the true you. So, perhaps beautiful flowers, herbs, some clear fresh water in a pretty cup, salt, symbols, candles and images that evoke a feeling of the sacred and a true sense of who you are becoming. Remember, being a spellcaster spiritually means connecting to the source. Your altar can reflect that.

For an altar, you simply need a space – it can be as large or as small as you wish. It's a beautiful place to keep oils and crystals, too. Images of inspirational people, mythological archetypes, Gods and Goddesses, you could include artists, poets, athletes, philosophers. What is important is that your altar and everything on it speaks to you, about you and who you wish to become. Rework your altar whenever you feel you have changed.

Magickal Tools

You may also wish to keep your magickal tools on the altar. Take your time collecting them. Here are some suggestions of tools you can place on your altar:

Cauldron: This is associated with all elements as it can hold all elements. It can be used for burning, for brewing potions, or for holding salt and earth. They have three legs and each leg represents an aspect of the triple Goddess: Maiden, Mother and Crone.

Wand: You can make your own wand, simply by collecting fallen wood from a tree you have a connection to. You can work with your wand to direct energy and to cast circle.

Chalice: Can be used to hold sacred or blessed waters.

Candleholder: Safe and beautiful, they are a wonderful Witches' tool.

Candlesnuffer: Some spellcasters prefer to staunch or snuff the candle, either between their fingertips or with a snuffer. This is believed to keep the energy with the spell, rather than blowing it away. I blow or snuff according to how the energy feels. I blow the candle out when I feel the energy needs to be sent out into the world.

Athame: The double-bladed Witches' knife is an important tool for working with energy. It can also be used to cast circle. Some spellcasters work with a sword, which is a stronger, more powerful delineator of where energy begins and ends. It is often used in energy surgery.

To Cast a Magick Circle

The casting of a protective circle is an important part of spellcrafting and magickal work. When we work magick, we enter into a slightly altered state of consciousness. It is very subtle for some, for others it can be almost a full trance. When in this altered state, we require protection from unwanted and sometimes unhealthy energies that can be attracted to our energy, from which these energies can feed. The casting of a circle delineates a world between the worlds, within which you can safely cast, craft, meditate, and do your magickal work. This protective boundary, through which no harm can enter and manifest, is your sanctuary and your safeguard.

The circle is cast in the direction called deosil. This means sunwise – and sunwise is in fact different in the northern hemisphere and the southern hemisphere. While the sun rises in the east in both hemispheres, and likewise sets in the west, the direction it appears to travel in is different. In the northern hemisphere, the sun rises in the east, then moves to the south (which is why the further south you go in the northern hemisphere, the warmer you get). In the southern hemisphere, the opposite applies – the sun rises in the east, then moves to the north.

This means that the deosil direction in the northern hemisphere is clockwise, and in the southern it is anti-clockwise. We cast, or open a circle, in the deosil direction so it flows with the natural energy of the planet.

(As an interesting aside, it also means that if clocks had been developed in the southern hemisphere they would have run in a different direction!)

Casting the Circle

There are many ways to cast a circle, from the very simple, to the very complex. Some spellcasters ensure they completely clear and bless the area in which they will work their spell before casting. Others simply begin, after finding a place where there is good energy. Most often we will be doing this at home – so we need to be prepared to work with the space we have.

The wonderful thing about circle casting is that it can be done almost anywhere. The energy and magick travels within you and you carry this ability to create a safe, powerful and magickal space wherever you go.

Stand facing the east. Raise your dominant or sending hand (the one you use to write with, or catch with), and extend it. (You may wish to use an athame or a wand or even a sword. I suggest beginning with your hand.) See (either in your mind's eye or with your imagination) a surge of energy extending in a line from your hand or your pointer finger. Now, you can choose the type of energy you are creating here, or as an exercise, you can see the quality of energy that naturally comes from you. Notice the colour your energy has. Your personal energy will have its own quality, and everyone's energy, and thus everyone's circle, is slightly different.

Remember to cast in the deosil direction. Standing on the spot, see this line of energy flow in a circle about you. Now turn so that it completely surrounds you, flowing out of you. Ensure the circle is joined. When your circle joins up, it is cast. You may wish to widen your circle so it extends above you, below you, and completely encloses you, becoming more of a sphere. Finally, your circle joins up.

Calling the Direction and Elements

Traditionally spellcrafters call in the directions and elements to join them in their magickal circle. It is a way of establishing where you are in the world and acknowledging the natural forces around you.

We also believe that there are guardians who care for each direction, looking after that part of the world, caring for the elements, creatures, energies and people that reside in that direction.

There are traditional directions where elements reside, and you can call them in from those, or you can call them in geocentrically. Geocentric just means according to the land where you are.

So, here are the traditional northern hemisphere directions and the elements associated with them. These are often referred to as correspondents. Types of animals, types of tools, and certain elements and energies are often considered to belong to each element.

Let's keep it simple to begin with and start with the elements.

East – Air

South – Fire

West – Water

North – Earth

However, if you live on the east coast of Australia, you may want to acknowledge the element that is actually most powerful according to that direction. So, your elements and directions may look more like:

East – Water (for the ocean)

North – Fire (as this is where it is warmest)

West – Earth (for the vast mountains and deserts that stretch to the west)

South – Air (for the great storms, the southerly busters that blow up the coast)

Whichever way you decide to cast, wherever you choose to acknowledge the elements and however you acknowledge the guardians of the directions, it is best to keep it simple at first. Over time, it can become richer, more personal, growing deeper. Initially, you can simply turn to face the direction, and say:

Hail and welcome Guardians of the East. I call upon the element of Water to join me in this circle now.

In time, you may want to add a few words about what water means to you, its cleansing abilities, and acknowledge any animals and deities associated with water who you would like to work with.

Try to align who and what you call in with the purpose and intent of your spells.

Remember to call to each direction and its element in turn, moving in a deosil direction to open. Circle casting nearly always begins in the east.

Following these simple steps can anchor and help you as you learn this art. The main point to remember and draw strength from is that you are firstly creating a protective boundary, then you are empowering it with magick by calling in the elements and directions, then you go about your work, safely and supported.

Closing the Circle

You will often see or hear closing the circle referred to as 'opening' the circle. In any case, when you have completed your work, you bring your circle down. If you don't, your spell can remain in place, unresolved, and the magick will not be fully sent out into the world. You can also drag some of the energy around with you throughout the day or night, and magick is best begun and completed, so there is a clarity about it. We must always end, or close, as we began – strong.

To close your circle, you turn to face the direction and element you last called. You're going to do exactly the same thing as you did when you cast your circle, only in reverse. So first you thank the last direction you called, thanking the guardians of that direction, thanking the element, and saying hail and farewell. Turn to the next direction, then the next, until you are at the east finally, and thank the guardians of the east, and the element that resides there. Then standing, see the energy all about and around begin to shimmer and fade in the reverse direction to which it was cast. This closing direction is known as widdershins. Some spellcasters extend their hand (or athame or wand) and draw the energy back into them. I am far more inclined to let it transmute and be closed so that the

energy can be absorbed into the world, rather than re-absorbed into me!

The Art of Magickal Dressing

When we work spellcraft it can help to look the part. Although it does not matter in some ways, in others, wearing certain clothes for certain practices can have a very real energetic impact.

There is the concept of robes. Now, you can be literal about this if you wish or you can think of the modern-day version I often see – the hoodie. If only hip hop artists and UFC fighters realised how much they looked like druids in their snug work-out hoodies! The point is that a strong cape with a hood is very handy for several reasons. It is weather protective, so if you are working outside it will have an impact in that you won't get wet or freeze while casting your spell.

Robes also provide a degree of anonymity – it's much harder to know who is outside at night working some magick when people cannot see you, your clothing, or even your size or body shape or hair colour! Robes cover you, shelter you and will help you feel very protected and strong. Also, if you choose to work with elements such as water, fire and air, obviously robes are going to help protect you.

A Link to a Magickal Past

Robes also link you right back to longstanding magickal traditions. When we see Witches or druids portrayed, they are often wearing robes. Somewhere along the line robes became more the domain of priests and monks, but the same principles apply. When we are doing certain sacred workings, we wear certain clothing (and sometimes no clothing at all – your choice). Everything plays a part in the power it will give you, and the energy it will promote or the energy it will suffocate. Some people just have one magickal 'outfit' they wear for special times when they want everything to be lined up perfectly for their spellcasting. For others it becomes a matter of nearly everything being magickal after a while. I'm kind of in that position myself now. It's harder for me to find clothing that doesn't have some kind of magickal memory attached to it. Because of how I live now nearly everything feels right to wear.

However, I do have some clothing that I wear for ritual work or spellcrafting alone, and it does have a certain energy to it and has held onto the magick. I can feel this energy every time I put that particular garment on. It adds a little extra energy to the whole ceremony and helps me make the mental shift from this world to the next.

The Magick of the Crown Covering

When we work magickally, it can be considered to be good protocol to have the head covered – or to reveal the head at the right time. This really is not about drama, or attempting to be theatrical, although having that cape or hooded robe really does put you in another frame of mind. Over time, as you do your magickal work, your robes will take on the energy of the working you've been doing. The more positive and successful your magick, the more of this energy your clothing will store. For some people this becomes more and more important over time.

The Magick of Personal Meaning

It's probably best you choose something that really has meaning for you to create your own magickal clothing. For example, magick practitioners will sometimes stitch symbols into their robes or a number of knots or stitches that have important personal symbolism to them.

Sometimes magickal people inscribe their magick onto their body in the form of magickal tattoos. The history of tattoos is that they were most often marks of ancestry or protection, and this always had magickal significance. However, it is not always necessary to mark the body permanently, unless that is something you have thought about and made a very serious and responsible decision about.

You can inscribe a symbol for the purpose and duration of a spell on your skin in a subtle place on your body, while you are undergoing the working and changing the energy into your life.

You can use body paint, or make your own out of clay or henna to create the magickal results you wish to manifest into your life. The materials you use will have an impact on the spell you are creating. If you are wanting a strong impact I would be inclined to really ground the energy with the earth from where you live, which will also hold your energy.

Amulets and Symbols

Magickal amulets and symbols were widely used in ancient cultures, such as Egypt and Mesopotamia. And you are not just tapping into the natural power, you're also having your spell fuelled by the thousands of years' worth of belief in them. Belief creates energy. We have never really stopped using spells and magick. We just kind of pretend we don't believe.

But watch people! Will they walk under a ladder? Will they step on a crack in the pavement? Humans are believers, and what we believe in has power. We've believed in spells for a long time, so when you cast and craft a spell you are tapping into an historic source of occult power.

Runic Symbols

Runes are and will be used in our magick. They are a form of written language developed by the people of the Norselands over 2000 years ago. They are symbolic and each rune holds within it many concepts and a great deal of energy. When you draw the rune on your skin or carve it into a candle you are really calling upon the energy held in the symbol to come to you to be of aid during your working. I do not feel you need to study the runes for years before you use them. However, working with respect and integrity is important – and also with humility. Symbols take time to learn, and one of the best ways to learn is to begin, have patience and develop your knowledge slowly and practically.

The Eye of Horus

One symbol you can begin to use right away is the Eye of Horus. This has been used for thousands of years as a symbol of protection, wholeness and health. It is wonderful to use if you are feeling rundown, hurt (emotionally and physically) or if you've been sick. If you have vague feelings of things being 'not quite right' the Eye of Horus or wedjat, can look out for you.

So, what is the Eye of Horus? In Egyptian cosmology (the way they believed the world and the planets and the whole natural thing to hold together) Thoth healed the God Horus, restoring his missing eye, giving him back his external and internal sight, and the gift of being able to 'look out' for danger and opportunities. (These things are not as different to each other as you would think.)

Eye of Horus Protective Talisman

This is a very ancient and effective spell for protection, a variation on an Egyptian spell, which we know an Egyptian woman named Helena cast around about 250 AD. This is a slightly more modern take, but the essence and power remain the same.

You'll need:

- *Parchment (a teeny-tiny piece)*
- *A pen with deep blue ink*
- *A little bottle – or a tiny glass tube*
- *Some string or pretty velvet thread*

What to do:

On the piece of parchment or thick paper, with deep blue ink, write, small as can be:

Heal me
Look out for me
Warn me
Encourage me
Inspire me
Let all I see be Clear
Give me no need to Fear

Keep me safe from all Harm
With this, my wedjat talisman charm
Bless me, and protect me, Horus

Hold the bottle in your hands for a moment and really feel the protective love and energy of the Eye of Horus and say the words you have written down out loud three times with strength and conviction. Really give it some energy and intensity, so the energy and certainty you bring to your spell is infused into the parchment and the words go out into the Universe and Horus can hear you!

- Then draw the eye of Horus on the other side of the small piece of parchment.
- Roll this parchment up and pop it in the little bottle, tie the velvet ribbon or thread about the neck of the bottle and wear it about your neck or wrist for nine days.
- When you have done this, you may hang it at the door of your room, within your locker, or off your bed – wherever you feel you most need protection and the magickal eye looking out for you.

- If you feel very seriously that you have suffered too much bad luck or that you are fragile, consider drawing the eye of Horus on your body. The best place for this is on your back, or between your shoulder blades, so literally Horus will 'have your back'. Ask a friend to help you.
- It is wise to say thank you to Horus often. Simply say, 'Thank you, Horus, for your watchful eye of protection'. It will reinforce the spell and re-energise it, boosting its power and increasing your own belief and conviction in your safety. That way, of course, your energy keeps on shifting and getting clearer, sounder, healthier and stronger, thus the safer and more protected you will be.

Creating a Sacred Spellcasting Space

Have you ever walked into a room or entered someone's shop or even a park or garden and just felt a sense of comfort, rightness and inspiration? These spaces make you feel like you want to stay there a while. Then there are spaces that have nothing 'wrong' with them at all but the energy feels 'off'. This feeling can exist even when a room or space is filled with all the right 'spiritual stuff' too – when the energy isn't working, no amount of crystals and purple velvet is going to fix this.

With this in mind, wherever you are going to do your spellwork needs to have that magickal, supportive, helpful and healthy vital energy. You need to feel great when you walk into the space. Having an outdoor space with the right energy that suits you is generally easy to find if you make sure it is safe and secluded enough for you to do your work. But some days it's going to be cold or raining or both and you're going to need a space indoors. Here are some easy and fun ideas to help you create a space that will make you feel magickal.

Make your Space Personal

Placement and space management is a magickal art that can be as simple as walking into a room and knowing that if you tidy up, clear the space and play different music, rearrange some objects and recharge what you love, everything will have a different energy. Adjust things in the space to suit you and you alone.

Creating a sacred spellcasting space is all about finding, creating and maintaining an environment in which you feel safe, comfortable, stimulated and peaceful and, most importantly, deeply connected. The space needs to be uplifting enough so that you don't feel so calm you sleep, nor so stimulating that you feel edgy and scattered. Many people are sensitive to the atmosphere of their space and will intuitively pick up on what is out of balance within an area. This intuition is something that comes naturally to magickal people. Always look after your sacred space. To me, energy shifting and working in a space is as routine as taking out the garbage and all that other stuff that we need to do. Doing magickal work creates debris and energetic leftovers so make sure you work to clear this debris out of your magickal space and your life.

When to Clear your Magickal Space

If you feel there is something not quite right in your space, clear it right away. If you are a planner and a practical person at heart, you could do it on a regular basis. It is a fantastic idea to get into a magickal 'housekeeping' routine. Here are some powerful times to do this magickal work.

- Use the waning moon to move energy out, especially strong energies that feel really glued in and very stuck.
- Use the new moon to bring beautiful new energies in. It is the best time for a blessing of a room or a house.

- A full moon is a powerful amplifier of energies. For me, I tend to clear a little before working with the full moon energy, as it is so strong. I am more inclined to do my magickal workings during the full moon, rather than clear and bring in during it.

The Ripple Effect

Whatever you do in your magickal space is going to have an impact on everyone around you. It will send out a kind of ripple effect that will be felt in many other areas. This ripple effect will be a little more contained in your magickal space, but it's a kind of energetic bath for your space that renews, invigorates and maintains the mental, physical and spiritual health of everyone within your home, or wherever you've chosen to create your space. It also increases the wonderful experiences, people and prosperity drawn to you.

A space can simply be imbued with energetic debris of past occupants and incidents, and the energy with which the room or home was created can certainly be felt many years after the original work has been done. The land on which a space is built will also bring its influence to bear on the atmosphere of a home. Essentially, many dilemmas or problems for occupants can be solved in peaceful, loving ways that have spiritual integrity at their core.

There can be rooms in which you feel extremely light-headed and faint in certain areas. You may also notice that in some rooms, homes, even suburbs, it's the people who live there who create the energy imbalances. If people are very unhappy or have lived lives in which they have had big problems to overcome or are ill or bitter or just plain nasty, their energy can leak outwards, hanging like an energetic cloud. Regardless of the source of the energy, clearing, cleansing and rebalancing works.

It's also a great idea to have a cleansing and energy clearing when you move into a new home. This is an important part of establishing your space as your own. The energy in a space does not need to be banished, but it needs to hold and emanate the essence of your personal energy, otherwise it may continue supporting the wishes and intentions of people who are no longer present.

White Candle Space Clearing Spell

Enter the space you wish to clear. Be sure you can be alone for about 20 minutes. This spell works best with as few external influences about as possible.

You'll need:

- A white candle
- Some salt for sprinkling
- Blessed water

What to do:

- Take the white candle and sprinkle the salt around it in a widdershins direction. This is for clearing and banishing.
- Light the candle and let it burn down. As it does, know its flame is burning through all energetic debris, leaving your space clear, calm, bright with potential.

- When the candle has burned down, collect the wax and salt, and bury them in the ground. Sprinkle more salt and blessed water over where it is buried, to keep the energy safe and transmuting below the ground.

How to Make a Smudge Stick

This is an old magickal practice that exists all over the planet. So, when you work with smoke and clearing you are joining a long line of magickal practitioners in shifting and moving and transmuting unhealthy energy.

You'll need:

- Fresh herbs. You can choose from any kind, but they need to be fresh and in lengths, not pre-dried and pre-cut. These are readily available. Of course, it is always best if you grow your own.

All herbs have different qualities:

- *Basil* is a herb that creates a great environment for students, strong memory and clear thinking.

- *Grandfather Sage* is a powerful and traditional clearer of negative energy.
- *Lavender* soothes and calms, and creates a nurturing, wise space. Wonderful to use if there are sleep disturbances.
- *Marjoram* is enriching and invigorating. Marjoram increases your ability to think clearly.
- *Rosemary* helps to clear, but also reinforces positive memories and helps you make wise choices.
- *Thyme* is a herb associated with faery energy, wellness and has a lively, revitalising energy.

Dry the herbs by hanging lengths of the herb in a space that is dry and well ventilated. It's lovely and is a beautiful energy boost too. Wrap string or ribbon around the ends of the herbs, knot it three times, leave a little bit of length in the string and tie the herbs so they hang upside down.

After three days, take down your herbs and wrap them tightly at the base, slightly looser along the length with a pure thread such as cotton or silk.

Carefully light the end, and then staunch it so there's no flame, just smoke. Always have some water handy in case a spark lands somewhere!

Walk through the house or sacred space widdershins holding your smudge stick, fanning the smoke out into the space before you. Pay particular attention to areas where the energy feels stuck, or unpleasant.

You need not burn the whole smudge stick down – just use enough so that you have smoked out the unpleasant energy.

The Spells

Protection Spells

We all have people and special keepsakes which we want to protect. We also need to protect ourselves from time to time. You'll find here several tried and well tested spells – they'll break curses and shield you from negativity, repel attacks and keep you from harm. Treat these spells like your rainy day clothes, or a crash helmet. They go a long way to ensuring you'll get through a risky time, safe and sound, body and soul.

Spells also work on a psychological level. What this means is that they give us the means and confidence to take steps to protect ourselves. Thus, our energy shifts and we are no longer attracting the same kind of negative behaviour.

A Spell to Heal an Argument

You'll need:

- To mend a friendship with a woman, you will need a yam, rounded in shape
- To mend a quarrel with a lover, use a pear
- To mend heartbreak after unfaithfulness, use an apple
- To mend a friendship with a man, use a yam, long
- A spoonful of honey
- Some green thread
- Some red thread

What to do:

- Open your circle.
- Call upon the Goddess Hina to mend friendships.
- Slice your fruit or yam lengthwise.
- Say:

This is our quarrel, our sadness, our parting

- Anoint the centre of each slice with honey and say:

Let misunderstanding end

- Join the two halves together again, letting the honey act as glue, and say:

Let sweetness join us once again

- Take a green thread and bind the two halves together, wrapping your choice of fruit or yam nine times.
- Take a red thread and bind the two halves together, wrapping the fruit or the yam nine times, saying:

Let love between us grow strong once again

- Place the fruit or the yam in the oven set at 180 degrees Celsius, until softened.
- Eat the fruit with cream or honey to taste. For the yam, sprinkle it with salt and enjoy with some soy sauce and garlic for purification of the relationship. Know that the sweetness of your meal is the growing return of love and good feelings between you both.

- With the food in your belly, make contact with your friend and let them know that you are sorry you have quarrelled, and that you wish to have them returned to your life. Leave the outcome to the God and the Goddess, and know their response is for your highest good.
- Close circle and may your friendship or love, if it is meant to be, be reborn.

Dark Moon Bath Blend

Blend and bless this at the sunset of a dark moon. This blend will release, remove and dissolve ties that you may have to difficult people and give you the strength to let go of those you find yourself unable to let go of. It is powerful and it will clear energies.

You'll need:

- Sea salt or glacier salt – your choice
- Frankincense resin or oil
- A small handful of juniper berries
- A bay leaf
- An oak leaf
- A small handful of sage
- Sandalwood and orange
- A piece of black tourmaline
- A silver or dark-coloured bowl
- A banishing pentagram – this can be drawn over the blend or you can use an actual pentacle and lay it on the blend for about three minutes, drawing it in your mind's

eye in the banishing direction and energised with silver banishing pentagram

- A rowan or eucalypt stick

What to do:

- Place all in a bowl. Meditate on the banishing pentagram, then stir, widdershins, at least nine times with a rowan or eucalypt stick. Stir in multiples of three.
- Place a pinch in your wash to clear any energies remaining from clothes!
- Throw a few handfuls of the blend into the bath, soak, release, and be free! Work with this any time the emotional attachment and the desire arises to reconnect to those who are not good for you, or substances or situations that are not good for you. This will help you really overcome temptation, and be very healthy in your emotional/spiritual and physical choices – and of course, thinking more clearly and freely is also supported when you work with this blend.

Dark Moon Spell

You will need to cast this spell during a dark moon in order for it to be most effective. You are not ill wishing, you are dissolving, transmuting and casting off ties to those qualities.

You'll need:

- Black candle
- A piece of charcoal
- Some juniper berries
- A handful of salt
- A handful of lemon verbena

What to do:

- Open your circle.
- On the black candle, write the names of the traits and qualities in yourself you no longer wish to see in your life. It is best to focus on qualities you wish to change in yourself. The clearer you are, the more powerful this will be.

- Set up the black candle in a candleholder so it is secure and light it.
- Now, light a charcoal piece, and burn the juniper on it.
- Let the candle burn down completely. If you must leave the room, close the door behind you firmly. It is important to contain this energy.
- Store the melted wax with the salt and bury it in the garden or a pot of earth. Sprinkle the lemon verbena over the top.
- Close your circle.

Protection Stones and Shells

A long time ago, hag stones were not only considered to be the most wonderful way of 'seeing' the Otherworld (you peered through the hole and into the world beyond the veil) but they also were considered to have strong protective powers.

You'll need:

- A stone with a natural hole in the middle of it (keep a look out and you'll find one when the time is right)
- Shells with natural holes in them
- A piece of fishing line

What to do:

- Thread the stones and shells onto your fishing line. You can make it as pretty and appealing as you wish.
- Hang it outside the front door or the back door. The harmful energies will slip through the holes and into the world between the worlds, where they will be cared for.

Removal of Psychic Attack

This spell is to be cast at the waning moon or the dark moon for the removal of psychic attack.

You'll need:

- A teaspoon of dried juniper berries
- A bay leaf
- A piece of dragon's blood
- A ground cinnamon stick
- Rosemary, dried or fresh
- Some charcoal discs
- A cauldron or fireproof container
- Athame (optional)

What to do:

- Go to your sacred space. Don't wash. Don't try to feel good. Be real. Be authentic.
- Cast your circle.
- Sit down. Please, don't ask for protection at this stage. You

want everything to be very clean, open and clear.

- Bring into your mind and say out loud the qualities of those people who have hurt you either through intent or ignorance or lack of understanding.
- Combine your herbs and stir them widdershins. This is your banishing blend.
- Light the charcoal discs and place on a protective surface or your cauldron.
- Place the herbs on them and let them smoke. Scoop the smoke into your hands and move it about your body, moving your entire self through the smoke. Once this is done, stand and imagine anyone or anything you feel may have harmed you standing with you, cords extending from you to them. Blow the smoke towards them, and see the cords fade and dissolve as the smoke clears them.
- Now ask for the Goddess Brigid to come in and slice cords and do some energetic surgery to heal swiftly any wounds made during the releasing process. You may wish

to use your athame during this process, cutting through energetic cords as you are guided.

- Once you are finished, put out the burning herbs. Sit still and breathe until you feel calm and centred and clear.
- Close your circle.

Stop Spell

One of my first and most simple spells came from a very old book on magick. It told of an ancient way to peacefully stop another being from hurting you. Write their name on a piece of parchment and place it under the snow. The result? That particular person would be prevented from harming anyone.

I live in very hot, very sunny Australia and I wondered if a freezer would work just as well.

One day, after being pushed to my limit, I cleared my mind of my emotions and with love in my heart, I wrote a name on a piece of paper. I focused on keeping my mind clear and wishing this person only good as I placed the piece of paper into a glass of water and then into the freezer, and said:

By all the powers of three times three
I wish only good to come to thee
I wish thee well, strong and happy
And very far away from me

It worked, slowly, safely and in a very subtle way. We were not 'parted' but it was as if we never truly connected again – and the bullying I was experiencing ceased.

To Move a Disturbing Spirit or Entity Along

There are times when we can feel something in our environment, like a spirit or entity who just won't leave. Of course, you can cleanse and banish, but you can also make use of this traditional spell and make a spirit bottle and offer the being a new home so you and the spirit can peacefully co-exist.

You'll need:

- A large bottle
- Some feathers, twigs, dried flowers, wood, a crystal such as obsidian, and some cotton wool

What to do:

- Gently place your ingredients in a sizeable pretty bottle.
- Ask the spirit to come forward and when you feel their presence show them the new home you have created for them.
- Place the bottle in the garden or suspend it from a tree. Make sure it is secure! We do not want to harm this spirit.

- The lovelier you make it, the more likely your spirit will move from your space and into its new home. The comfier it is, the less you'll see it. Don't stopper the bottle.

Spells for Success, Power, and Abundance

Money is a very loaded subject in our culture. We want it, but we feel guilty about having it. We obtain it and we waste it. We think without it we are powerless. And we allow imaginary money – credit – to send us into debt. Money is a form of energy, and it represents what we have put our energy into – and money is energy we then pour into something. Over time, I have developed some very effective money spells to help us all have more power, success, independence and self-determination.

Simple Success Spell

This spell will leave you 'awash with success'.

You'll need:

- A beeswax candle
- Two tablespoons of honey
- A few pieces of citrine
- A small handful of dried mint

- A few marigold flowers
- A small handful of elderflowers and leaves

What to do:

- Carve an image of a little bee into your candle. Anoint your candle with a little of the honey, then drive the citrine pieces into the base, around the outside of the candle. While you are decorating your candle, run a warm bath.
- Light your candle and set it up near your bathtub.
- Sprinkle your prosperity herbs over the bathwater.
- Gaze at the waters and see the magick of the herbs moving into the water, and say:

Bee of honey
Bee of health
Bring to me deserved wealth
Bee of wisdom
Druid's bee
Bring prosperity unto me

- Say your name three times.
- Get into the bath. Think of all the good things you'll do with the prosperity coming your way. Rub the honey into your feet, your hands, your forehead, and know that your every footstep creates wealth and sweetness, as does the work of your hands, and the products of your thoughts. Wash the honey from you, but know that traces of its golden, sweet and sticky energy will cling to you, drawing success and money.
- Dry off, feeling abundant and brimming with good fortune.

Fortune and Fae Spell

Traditionally humans have gone to the faerie kingdom for help with health, healing and good fortune, as well as matters of love. I have found them to be very generous helpers.

On a waxing moon, head out at night. In a little cup, eggshell, leaf or nutshell, place some bread and honey and sprinkle with milk or cream. Hold it up for the faeries to see and sense. Call to them and offer them your service in cleaning up and caring for the environment. Ask them for assistance, and leave the offering out for the faeries!

Do this regularly and you will find money comes to you in lucky and very unexpected ways – just be sure to keep your word and clean up, recycle more and do regular litter pick-ups to keep the balance.

Plant a Money Tree

When I've travelled I've seen so many variations on the money tree. They're often found covered in coins, with symbols of blessings and longevity, like deer and turtles living in the branches – it's kind of a tree heaven where your every need is provided for! My money tree has always brought good fortune and prosperity.

You'll need:

- Somewhere to plant your money tree! Make sure it's positioned somewhere you will go every day. Give it plenty of room to grow as you prosper as the way you treat your money tree will influence your finances
- A healthy tree or a succulent plant for good fortune
- 10 gold coins
- 6 pieces of citrine
- Symbols of prosperity and good fortune, such as little coins tied to the ends of the branches, or toy animals that you love. Be inspired in your imaginings.
- Water blessed at waxing or full moon will have that energy

of expansion and increase! Be sure to gather some to offer to your money tree

What to do:

- Cast your circle.
- Dig a hole for your tree, feeling yourself clearing away and transforming all that separated you from your abundance.
- Sprinkle some blessed water into the hole.
- Touch the roots of the plant with the coins and the citrine, then put five of each into the hole for the plant. Before planting say three times:

From little things big things grow
Into this earth the coins are sewn
From rich soil and blessed water
I stand here now, Fortuna's daughter
(If you are a man, say
From this rich soil abundance comes
I stand here now, Fortuna's son)

- Plant your magickal money tree and fill in the hole with rich earth.
- Place five coins around the plant, and another piece of citrine, to inspire prosperity. Multiples of five stimulate change and a change in fortune is on its way.
- Close your circle.
- Be sure to nurture your plant with the certainty that you are abundant. Always share the wealth, in the form of helping others, and share the plant, as she will have many shoots and take root in many places!

High Tide of Psychic Power

This ritual bath salt blend will help really expand your power.

You'll need:

- A mortar and pestle
- Some frankincense resin
- Some jasmine resin
- A handful of salts – sea salt or glacier salt
- A small handful of jasmine flowers
- A few drops of frankincense oil
- A few drops of jasmine oil
- A few drops of sweet orange oil
- A cinnamon stick

What to do:

- Pound the resins to a powder in a mortar and pestle.
- Add these to the bowl along with the rest of the ingredients and stir deosil with a cinnamon stick, then store in an airtight jar. Use three tablespoons in your bath when you need some extra power and shine!

Money Drawing Oil Blend

This blend is a little messy and sticky – but it's effective and works quickly – money will literally stick to you.

You'll need:

- A few drops of bergamot oil
- A teaspoon of manuka honey
- A pinch of cinnamon, powdered
- A cinnamon stick
- A dark glass jar to store the money drawing blend (green is best)

What to do:

- Stir this blend up deosil with a cinnamon stick and store in a glass jar. Rub a little on your wallet, your money box, your calendar and diary. Dab a little on your wrists before applying for a job, or anytime you have money matters to discuss.

Money Management Spell

What you do with money when it comes to you is going to determine your future prosperity.

To reinforce your intent, take magickal action.

You'll need:

- 3 green ribbons
- 3 coins

What to do:

- When the moon is new, tie three green ribbons around a branch of a flowering tree.
- Bury 3 coins at the roots of the tree. When the tree flowers or shoots above that point where you have tied the ribbons, you will have made good use of your money and saved a little nest egg.

Harvest Spell

This spell is one of the oldest in my Grimoire and is simple and perfect for Lughnasadh, or any time you need to give thanks for blessings.

You'll need:

- A stick of vanilla incense
- A silver coin
- A piece of orange fabric
- Two green candles anointed with neroli oil
- Flowers and sprigs of fast-growing herbs to place on your altar

What to do:

- Sitting at your altar, light the incense. Take a silver coin and wrap it in the piece of orange fabric. Place this on your altar.
- Put two green candles anointed with neroli essential oil on either side of the coin wrapped in orange fabric. Light the candles. Concentrate on the silver coin and visualise your

dream coming true in the present, not at a future time. Say three times:

As the waves of the ocean are infinite
As the trees in the forest grow tall
Let my work now bring me to harvest
I'm ready to receive my all

- Shift your focus to the orange cloth and understand that harvest is coming. Blow out the candles, first right, then left, and place flowers and sprigs of fast-growing herbs around your magickal space.

Love Spells

They are innocent looking words, aren't they? Love Spells! Do not be fooled! This is powerful magick! One out of every two questions I am asked as a Witch is 'Can you cast a love spell for me?' Spells are times when we put aside a moment to practise loving…with every stitch of our charm pouch or use of rose petal, love stirs, awakens and grows within, and we send out that energy and draw it towards us.

So, to minimise backfiring, these spells are absolutely safe, loving and yet they are very serious in their intent. It's a good and worthy goal – to help bring more love into your life. Remember that when working love magick, free will is of the greatest importance. We do not cast to draw a specific person. Some of these spells are going to require more work. Others are simpler, less time consuming. You will know which to do.

Cards of Love

I recommend using one of my decks for this spell-reading, but any Oracle or Tarot cards you have and love working with will be perfect! So, we're going to work with the skill of divination for this spell. We're also going to call in a deity. I would suggest working with Aphrodite.

You'll need:

- Your Oracle or Tarot cards
- A couple of red candles
- Luscious red fabric for your altar
- Rose quartz, unpolished ruby or garnet for your altar

What to do:

Open your circle, light your candles and arrange your altar. Spread out the red fabric.

Shuffle the cards while contemplating your question. When you feel it is the right time, stop and cut the deck. If, for instance, you wish to uncover the blocks within a relationship, split the deck into three piles, turn one pile upside down, and put them back together again and reshuffle before dealing out the cards. This method is very effective for revealing where you're stuck, what you may not be aware of, or what you may be in denial about.

When you have put your deck together again, take three cards from the top of the deck and lay them out on the left in a horizontal line. Then take three cards and lay them out to the right, again in a horizontal line. Then take three more cards and lay the first above the lines, the second below the lines and the third to the right of the laid out cards.

The set of three cards on the left represents your partner or the person you feel a connection with. The first card you put down indicates their true feelings, the second how they behave towards you in public and the third how their feelings will develop.

The set on the right represents you. The first card, card four, indicates your true feelings, the second, card five, your public face and how you come across to this person, and the third, card six, the direction in which your own feelings will develop.

The card above these two groups, card seven, indicates the destiny of this relationship. The card below, card eight, indicates the potential problems, blocks and challenges and the lessons from this union. The card to the right, card nine, will give you guidance regarding right action in this relationship.

- Make notes about your reading in your Grimoire, and remember, you've asked for help, real help, and the cards do not lie. Take the advice of Aphrodite.
- Blow out your candles, making a wish on the out breath.
- Close circle.
- Thank Aphrodite for her assistance. Have confidence in her guidance.

Love Potion Tea

Tea is perhaps the simplest, most effective magickal potion there is. Remember your healing spell where you used lemon verbena? Now you can work with that plant for a relationship bliss tea.

You'll need:

Pluck leaves from your lemon verbena, only a third maximum at any time – the plant will flourish from a bit of clearing! Dry them by laying them out on a dry cloth in a place with good air circulation. Your altar is perfect – maybe just open a window slightly – you don't want the leaves blowing away! Once dry, you can put them in an airtight jar and keep them away from moist environments. Be sure to label them!

What to do:

- Use your hands to shred the dry leaves into little pieces. As you do so, say wonderful, soothing words over them… like 'luck', 'good fortune', 'bliss', 'effortless', 'joy', 'ease', 'flow', 'friend', 'companion'.

- Steep a small teaspoonful of leaves in a cup of just-boiled water. Stir them widdershins if you need to remove any bad feelings, and stir them deosil if you're ready for some new energy either in your current or a new relationship!
- Wait till the bliss tea is cool enough to sip, then drink it all up, maybe while writing in your Grimoire.

You can easily blend this herb with others for different effects.

- To bring in romance: two parts lemon verbena, one part rose petals
- To dream of love: two parts lemon verbena, one part lavender or a touch of mugwort, a herb which induces very insightful and vivid dreams. Only a touch, mind, it is powerful!
- To spice up your love life, to make it more fun: blend lemon verbena and orange zest
- To purify your love: lemon verbena and lemon zest
- To bring good cheer: lemon verbena and lime zest
- To improve your memory: lemon verbena and mint (good for those of us who forget anniversaries and other romantic dates!)

Make a Magickal Love Charm

This charm pouch will gently, safely yet strongly attract love. Create this powerful little charm on a Friday, the day named for Freya, the Norse Goddess of love, and also sacred to Aphrodite, the Greek Goddess of beauty, independence and love.

You'll need:

- A red cloth heart
- A piece of red velvet or silk, large enough to make a small pouch, around 20 cm square will be perfect
- A few cloves
- A small handful of dried orange peel
- A small handful of dried rose petals
- A cinnamon quill (or powdered cinnamon is fine)
- A small piece of rose quartz or an unpolished ruby or a piece of garnet (each of these has slightly different energy. You choose which works best for you)
- Red cotton and a needle
- A red ribbon

What to do:

After dedicating this working to all that is love, ask for Freya's or Aphrodite's blessing for this charm.

- Take your cloth heart and breathe deeply into it seven times. Whisper words such as the things you wish to have and wish to be. Stay in the energy. Let any sceptical thoughts drift by.
- When you have finished charging this heart, place the love-energy charged heart at the centre of the red velvet or silk.
- Then gently cover the heart with your ingredients – the orange for sweetness, joy, health in love, the rose for truth and beauty, the cinnamon for spice and sensuality and the cloves for purification and healing. Place the crystal or gemstone on last.
- When you have completed this, breathe a wish into the pouch. Gather up all the ends of the fabric, and stitch it with needle and thread into a little pouch. Sew the pouch together then tie it firmly with the red ribbon. Tie this three times, saying each time:

By the power of three times three
As I do will, so mote it be

- Hang this magickal pouch over your bed, keep it tucked under your pillow or wear it under a special outfit. Give it time. Your love is on their way.
- You must remember that when you are working love magick, free will is of the greatest importance. We do not cast to draw a specific person. This is a powerful, emotional, volatile area, so it must be treated with great respect.

Beltane Garland

Beltane is the old Celtic and Witches' festival of love and fertility and commitment. This spell can be cast at any time of the year to draw love.

You'll need:

- Three pieces of a vine-like flowering plant, something really flexible and about a metre long — jasmine is perfect
- Some long-stemmed herbs such as rosemary or lavender
- Roses, gardenias, any flowers that you love
- Some little bells, ribbons, fabric

What to do:

- Braid the vines, just as you would hair. The braid does not have to be tight – keep it loose and soft, but firm enough so they are woven together. As you do so, chant softly:

Through this circle love enters anew
Worthy, heartfelt, pure and true

Steadfast, honest, lasting, kind
Into this garland I now bind

Twist or tie the ends of the plait together so you have a beautiful circle. Now thread the herbs through the garland. Add the flowers. Tie some bells onto the vines to get the faeries involved. They are wonderful allies when it comes to love!

Once you've finished, staying in that strong, loving energy, hang the Beltane garland on your front door. The best times are when there is a new to full moon, or on a Friday, or best of all, at Beltane, the traditional day for love and passion in the Witches' calendar, 30 April–1 May in the northern hemisphere or 31 October–1 November in the southern hemisphere.

Self-love Spell

This spell will help you break through barriers, eliminating negative thought patterns you've held on to about yourself. Do this with all of your heart and watch the changes begin.

You'll need:

- A private space and some alone time for at least an hour
- A large mirror
- Clay (you can purchase really gorgeous refined white and pink clays, or you can get very earthy about this and collect your own clay.)
- A beautiful red piece of cloth for your altar
- A picture of yourself that you like – better still, one you love
- A little bit of your hair
- A candle for your altar

What to do:

Open your circle. Once you've cast your circle, take off your clothes. Standing skyclad before the mirror, really see your body.

Allow yourself to see the beauty and perfection of all that you are, no matter how 'imperfect' you may judge yourself to be.

- Take the clay and cover the part of your body you have negative or critical thoughts about. Clay draws out impurities so really feel it drawing out of you all criticisms, all negative thoughts, all the physical negativity that may have held you back from being healthy and comfortable, loving and accepting about your own body.
- When you feel the energy reach a peak, take yourself to the shower, turn on the water hard, and really know that along with the clay running down the drain so too are all the old fears and doubts and self-criticisms. They're history! You are worthy of love, self-love, love of others. You deserve respect. Stand tall, as tall as you can under the water. Let this belief flow right into you.
- Step out of the shower and dry yourself off with a beautiful, soft towel.
- Go back to your room or sacred space.

- Take your red cloth, and make a little altar. Place on this your picture of yourself, and around this place your hair. If you have short hair that's okay, just pop a little about. Light a candle on the altar.
- Now, to the picture of yourself, and to you, say out loud:

I love my body, it is beautiful and strong
I love my mind, it's clear and clever
I love my spirit, it's bright and high
I love my feelings, they're human and heartfelt
I love myself exactly as I am right now

Close your circle. Snuff out the candle. Shake yourself a little, and put on some music that is uplifting and eat something sweet to ground you. For the next seven days put a little clay on whatever part of your body you feel critical about. Within one lunar cycle, you'll be more grounded in your self-love. You will believe you are beautiful and worthy of love, and you will shine.

Dreaming of Love Pillow

Magickal pillows are fantastic tools. They smell beautiful, hold power and you sleep on them all night, so that they're working while you're resting. It also means the magick can get in deep because we are highly open to magick and energy while we sleep.

You'll need:

- A handful of rose petals
- A handful of dried jasmine
- Some sprigs of rosemary
- A bay leaf
- A few peppercorns
- A little sprinkle of lavender flowers
- A little sprinkle of chamomile, if you wish
- Deep red thread and a needle
- Parchment and a pen with crimson or purple ink
- A few drops of essential oils – choose from lavender, rose, rosewood, rose geranium, patchouli
- Soft, lovely deep red fabric

Note: If you'd like to get really funky, pop in a small piece of dried mango wood. You can find them in Indian stores and they're renowned for their love-drawing magick.

What to do:

Friday is perfect but if that's not possible, any evening will do, especially an evening around 7 pm when the moon is new through to full. I would not recommend doing this spell when the moon is waning.

- Gather all the flowers, herbs and the peppercorns, and stir them together in a bowl – you can use the mango wood for this. If you have a cauldron to work with, even better.
- Take your parchment. Write what it is you would love from a relationship and let the words flow. Write your name down frequently and often, too. Then, sprinkle your essential oil onto your parchment.
- While all the ingredients are brewing away, stitch your pillow and with every stitch say a word to do with what you want in a relationship. It could be 'depth' 'fun'

'conversation' 'adventure' 'passionate kisses'. Remember that with every stitch you are filling your pillow case with love-attracting energy. Leave one short side open so you can fill your pillow.

- Pop in all your herbs and spices and stitch up the final side, saying as you do so:

With every stitch
My spell is true
My true love now
I dream of you

(Needles and pins are very magickal objects that really 'stick' the energy into the object, driving it in.)

- Pop this under your pillow. Your true love will become more and more aware of you. You may even dream of them tonight…

Love Goddess Spell

You'll need:

- A pink, red or orange candle
- A heart talisman (you can find lots of these on eBay or in op shops or use an old piece of jewellery. It's really wonderful if it has some connection to you personally)
- Rose petals
- One pink, red or orange charm pouch

What to do:

- On a Friday, go to your altar, and cast your magick circle.
- Using your index finger, cast a circle of light around yourself, tracing it in the air.
- See a beautiful circle of white light protecting, balancing and energising you and your magickal space.
- Call in each of the elements, saying:

I welcome the spirits of the earth, air, fire and water to this circle.
Blessed be!

- Take your candle, and anoint it from top to bottom, then carve your name into it along with the word 'love'.
- Take your candle and hold it to your heart. Feel the love in your heart and pour it into your candle, activating your love energy, ready to be set alight and sent out into the world. Say:

By Rhiannon, Ishtar and Aphrodite
I now ignite my love energy
By all the power of three times three
As I do will, so mote it be

- Feel your heart's powerful alluring energy of love and desirability pouring into your candle. Place it on the altar and light it, feeling your attractiveness come even more alive.
- Next, take your heart talisman and hold it to your own heart. Say:

By Rhiannon, Ishtar and Aphrodite
A loving heart I draw to me
By all the power of three times three
As I do will, so mote it be

- Place your talisman heart on your altar with the pink candle. As you do so, feel the power of your love Goddess spell radiating its energy out into the world, an ambassador for your heart.
- Take your rose petals in your hand, and hold them to your heart. Say:

By Rhiannon, Ishtar and Aphrodite
A love so sweet now comes to me
By all the powers of three times three
As I do will so mote it be

- Place your rose petals on your altar beside your talisman heart and your candle. As you do so, understand that whoever shall come to you now is for the highest good of all concerned and that this love will serve your happiness.
- Stand with arms outstretched and feel the energy of the planet's unconditional love pouring into you, lighting up your every cell, activating all your potential for true love.

- Say out loud in a strong clear voice three times:

I am a beautiful, desirable being.
I am worth loving. I love. I am loved. I love. I am loved

- When your candle has burnt down, take its wax, your heart talisman and your rose petals. Place all three together in your charm bag. Tie the cord three times. As you do so, say:

Bound around this spell shall be
By all the powers of three times three
My true love now comes to me
As I do will, so mote it be

- Thank and farewell the elements, and close your magick circle by pointing your index finger in the direction you began in, tracing your circle in the opposite direction to close, drawing the beautiful energy of the circle back into you.
- Ground yourself by eating an apple, the fruit of Aphrodite.

- Carry your charm bag on you for the rest of Friday's daylight hours.
- On Friday evening, take your heart talisman out of its pouch and wear it around your neck or tuck it into your clothing for at least one week. You may wear it longer if you wish, but be sure to wear it until the following Friday until the same time you put it on to fully activate its magick.

A Ritual Bath to Draw Love

Friday nights are sacred to Aphrodite and to Freya, and a great evening to recharge your self-love.

Firstly, light a candle and get out your Grimoire. You can write down all your musings about the relationship within its pages. Spend time really noticing your good points and affirm to yourself that you are worth loving, and worthy of attracting a wonderful relationship into your life now.

Run yourself a warm bath, light a pink candle and sprinkle seven drops of rose absolute, rose otto, rose maroc or rose geranium essential oils into the bathwater.

While bathing by candlelight, think of all the qualities you would like in a partner – it's important and essential to contemplate what you want, not who you want, in this exercise!

Afterwards, put on a beautiful outfit and eat an apple – they're sacred to Aphrodite. Stay really 'cushioned' in that place of love, feel it soothe, heal and re-energise you.

Once you're in bed, there is room for nothing except blissful, loving thoughts.

This could be a good time, too, to pop a Dreaming of Love Pillow beneath your regular pillows.

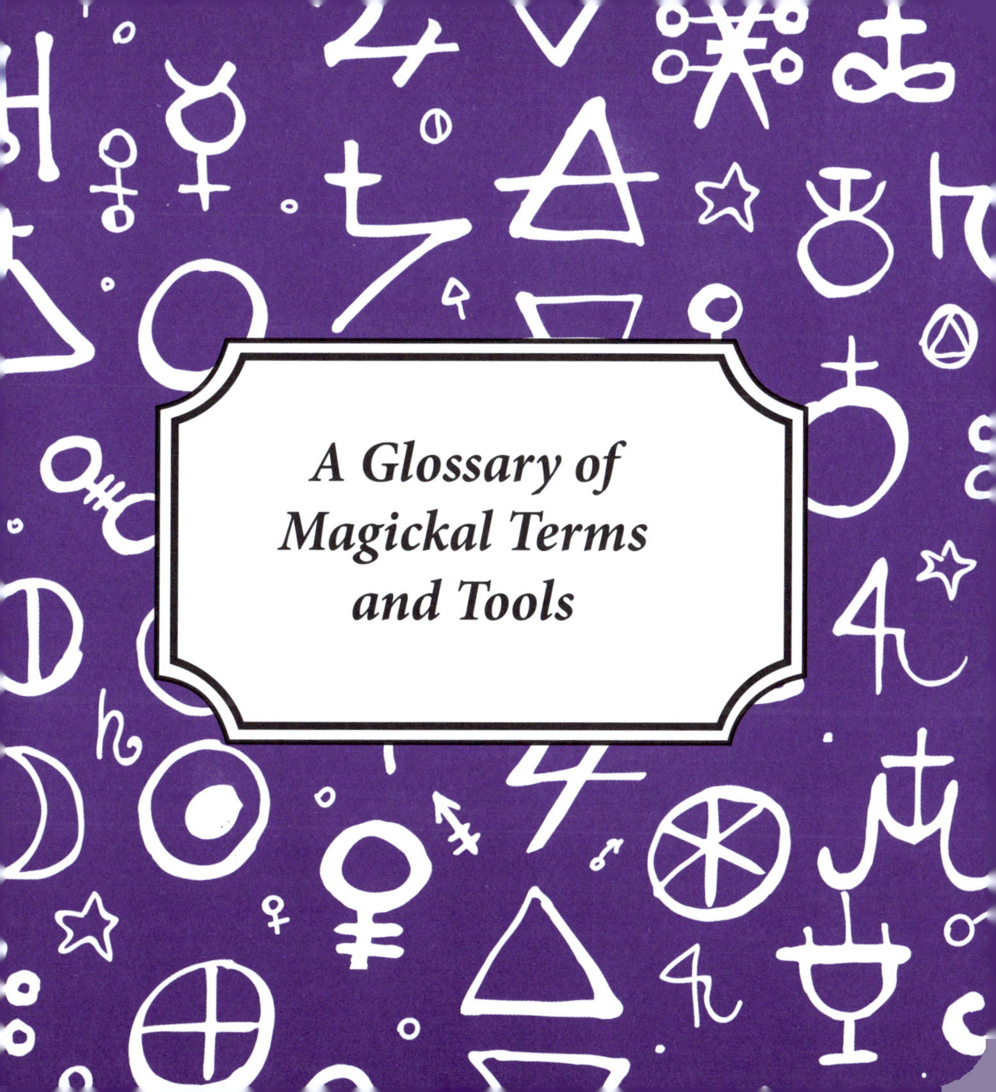

A Glossary of Magickal Terms and Tools

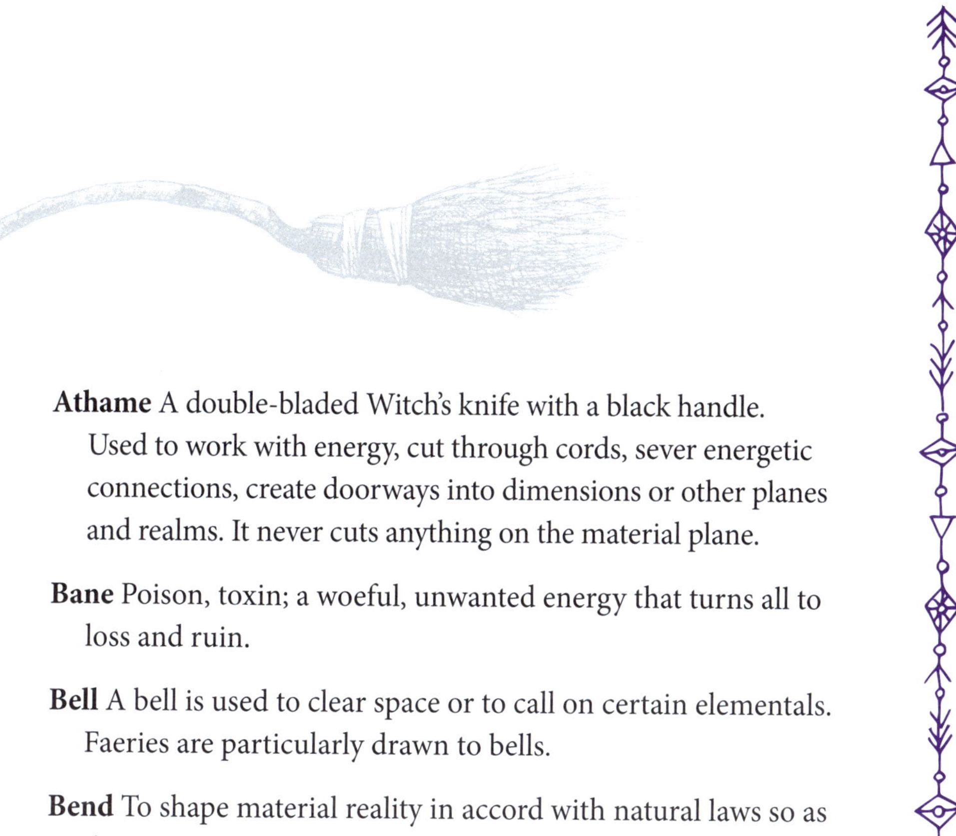

Athame A double-bladed Witch's knife with a black handle. Used to work with energy, cut through cords, sever energetic connections, create doorways into dimensions or other planes and realms. It never cuts anything on the material plane.

Bane Poison, toxin; a woeful, unwanted energy that turns all to loss and ruin.

Bell A bell is used to clear space or to call on certain elementals. Faeries are particularly drawn to bells.

Bend To shape material reality in accord with natural laws so as they merge with the will.

Bind To magickally restrict the potential or urge to harm or hurt.

Black magick Whether magick is evil or malicious or kind or healthy is really about the purpose of the spell and the intention of the caster. There is no black or white – it is all about the focus and energy of the intention and action.

Candle magick A form of magick that works with flame and light. Candles are dedicated to a particular purpose, and the burning of them activates the spell.

Cauldron A cast-iron, three-legged Witch's cauldron can be used to cook, brew potions, or hold fire for a ritual.

Cast The action of sending out magick.

Cast a circle To create a circular space of protection, healing. A world between the worlds, in which magick can safely be practised, a threshold that contains magick in a safe space, a threshold across which negativity cannot pass.

Charmstone A stone or crystal that has been blessed and charged with energy for a magickal purpose. It can then be held, dipped in water, or touched to pass the blessing or the magick along. It is a traditional practice in Scotland, Ireland, Northern England, Iceland, and amidst the indigenous tribal peoples of the Americas.

Circle A gathering of Witches or spiritually inclined people. The circle is formed in order to avoid hierarchy. Circles are without beginning and end, top or bottom.

Colour magick Hues hold vibration and have an energetic, psychological and physiological impact on us. Colours can add magick to all our spells, and help hold the magick in place.

Black: For banishing – tie your ribbon during the waning moon, or when the weather turns colder and winter begins to make her chilly presence felt.

White: For spiritual assistance – increasing intuition, for example.

Red: For passion and love.

Blue: For harmonious communication and friendship.

Green: For growth and connection to nature, healthy bodies and minds.

Purple: Royalty, higher states, connection to All.

Curse Ill-wishing, purposely desiring harm to another, and taking steps to achieve this.

Deosil Sun-wise. In the northern hemisphere, this is clockwise, as the sun rises in the east and moves to the south. Sun-wise in the southern hemisphere is anti-clockwise – as the sun rises in the east, and moves to the north. This direction is expansive, opening, and a calling in.

Grimoire An instruction book of magick and spellcraft that contains the personal notes and rites of magicians, Witches, or magickal practitioners.

Hail A term of greeting, as in Hail and Welcome. Directions, elements, Goddesses and Gods are often greeted this way when circle is cast.

Pendulum The use of a crystal or weight attached to a chain or thread, which is 'asked' to provide yes or no answers. The pendulum swings in the direction of the answer.

Pentacle The pentacle is a Pythagorean form, a five-pointed star enclosed within a circle. It represents earth, air, fire, water and spirit in balance.

Potion A potion is a kind of drink that is made with magickal intentions and magickal ingredients, for a specific purpose. They can also work on a vibrational level and include sacred or blessed waters.

Ritual A ceremony with a particular order and set structure, often with several participants. Magickal rituals are often held to celebrate the Wheel of the Year and its festivals, to raise

energy for healing, or to create, experience and activate the sacred.

Runes An ancient Nordic system of stark, linear symbols that have mundane, philosophical and oracular meanings and significance. Runes can be worked with to enhance spellwork, attract energy, and protect the user from harm. They form a true body of magickal work.

Scry The art of divination through gazing, such as when the gypsy stares into a crystal ball. Scrying can also be performed by entering a light trance and staring into fire, a still body of water, clouds, or a dark piece of glass. It is an ancient art which shifts perception in order to receive messages from beyond the human realm.

Skyclad Nudity in spellcraft, rituals or magick. Not sexual, but a way of deeply entering into nature, and being utterly revealed, vulnerable, transparent – and free.

Tarot A divination system using cartomancy featuring 78 cards, divided into three sections: the Major and Minor Arcana and the Court cards. There are four suits with prescribed meanings. With its mysterious origins, the Tarot is a gateway into archetypes, a complete system of magick and an effective way of predicting events and outcomes.

Wand A wand directs energy and can be made of wood, bone, stone, iron or crystal. They have their own energy and are often used to cast circles to heal or to pour energy into an object or a person.

Widdershins To direct against the sun – the opposite direction to deosil. In the northern hemisphere this is anti-clockwise – from east to north, to west. In the southern hemisphere it is from the east, to the south, to the west, then to the north again. We cast circle or work or stir in this direction to clear, banish and separate, or to close or unwind a circle that has been cast for group or solo spellwork.

About the author

Lucy Cavendish is an internationally acclaimed spiritual author and intuition expert. She exhibited strong extra-sensory abilities as a child, and with no answers from school or mainstream religion, Lucy set out on a personal quest to understand and develop her magickal gifts. Lucy grew up in Sydney, Australia, and she has lived in Paris, London and the United States. When she's not writing or speaking, you'll find Lucy surfing in the ocean, wandering deep within a faery forest, or dancing with the spirits in an ancient stone circle.

For more information visit www.lucycavendish.com.au